Let It Brew

Urmi Trivedi

Foreword

With deep grace of God, this work is seeing a physical form. This book follows the same theme as my first book "Over a Cup of Coffee". It is based on interesting discussions, conversations and musings with the intention of self-reflection. I feel "Let it Brew" will continue to help me explore and live in the question. I hope this effort inspires the readers.

I am deeply grateful to my family – my daughter Ashna, my husband Pranav, my parents Dr. Gita and Dr. Prafullakumar Gumashta, my brother Dr. Anurag, my in-laws Raksha and Dr. Bhupen Trivedi and my sis-in-law Dr. Ranak and Vibhor Chhabra and dear Ria for their love and support. I am grateful to life, friends and colleagues for giving me the experiences that I can pen and I am grateful for amazing authors and gurus who keep inspiring me to uplift myself.

I am thankful to my editor Karen from Create Space

With deep humility, I present this to my God Krushna.

Urmi Trivedi
Urmi.trivedi0@gmail.com

This book is dedicated to my daughter Ashna

and my parents Dr. Gita and

Dr. Prafullakumar Gumashta

Topics

1. You Are Not a Tree
2. Best Day Ever
3. Modes of Silence
4. Fill your Life
5. Heal your Life
6. Clean your Life
7. Empty the Boat
8. Unhurried ways
9. The Mandala
10. Do the Things that Make You Gasp
11. The $10M Check
12. Worry Free Diet
13. Let Your Heart Be Light
14. Cut it Out!
15. Love Your Neighbor, but First Love Yourself
16. Ten Thousand Ears
17. The Practice of Forgiveness
18. Let the Loop Run Itself Out
19. The Feeling of Self Reliance
20. The Tyranny of Should
21. Innocence and Ignorance
22. Tough Lives of God
23. Not Who But Why
24. Identity Crisis
25. What are You Going to Do Less of and More of?
26. Leave the Driving to Greyhound
27. Courage and Resilience
28. Gratitude Journal
29. Conditions for Happiness
30. No Big Deal

1. You Are Not a Tree

The thought of this topic was inspired by a quote by Jim Rohn: *"If you don't like where you are, change it. You are not a tree."* Really, change it. Why are we so afraid of new things and change? Why do we always use practicality as an excuse to avoid change and keep suffering through it? Why do we behave like trees?

A few months ago, as I neared the hundred-day mark of my job hunt, one of my beloved advisors said, "Maybe you should have stuck around and found something before you quit." Another one asked me, "Can you not go back?" I guess they believe being in an uprooted stage is not fun. However, if I want to change, I must uproot myself to find the soil and environment that facilitates growth. I didn't uproot myself to go back, and I needed the gift of time to find the correct soil.

On the other hand, I am blessed to have friends and family watching my journey and reminding me to focus on one step at a time. The universe will automatically send something my way, and it has. I know it, and I believe it. The lesson that I need to keep learning is that of patience. Once we uproot ourselves, it takes time. I always focus on the big picture. Today I am itching to find out what's next, but down the road, I will fondly look back at this time and thank God for giving me the courage and granting me the luxury of time.

As I think about how I am not a tree, I am reminded of the saying, "You only live once." So why should we live in a state of dissatisfaction and unhappiness? Why can't we have the courage to get inner peace?

The universe always tests our intentions. It tests whether or not we are true to our beliefs. Some of us have tougher tests than others. Once we prove we are serious, I feel confident fate will turn in our favor. The universe helps us to find the best version of ourselves, so sometimes it tests us over and over again. It pushes us to change and forces us to "not be a tree."

So, for me, if I am unhappy, I am not a tree, and I will push for change. I will not let fear of failure or fear of being in an uprooted state stop my efforts. However, I will plan my time. I will trust the universe, and I will reflect on the lessons it wants me to learn and remember.

I have left you with love And I am not coming back

I have a new journey to undertake

And I am walking ahead

The days may be tough

And I may get lonely

But hope and faith will get me there

I have things to learn, I have paths to try

Don't hold me back

I have just one life and now is the time

I have no regrets

I will follow my dream, I will find my bliss

I have something to share

2. Best Day Ever

The credit for this topic goes to my five-year-old, Ashna. Summers are a lot of fun for her. She enjoys playing out till late, especially with the scooter and on the splash pad. These days I often hear her say, "I had the best day ever." It sure doesn't take much to please little kids! As the saying goes, *"Enjoy today as this is the only time you will get to live it."*

I have a lot to learn from this. Everyday could be the "best day" in some aspects. Either our expectations are too high for the best day ever, or we haven't defined our best day ever, or we have an attitude of finding faults. I have often heard people say, "It was a wonderful day, but it was too hot." Why can't we just stop at "It was a wonderful day"? Let's think: What will our best day look like? Is it that lazy day spent on a beach, enjoying nature's magnanimous style? Is it spending time with our most loved ones and talking about life experiences? Is it connecting to the divine in a way that we haven't experienced before?

I enjoy asking myself: How am I feeling at this moment? Do I say I am feeling blissful, anxious, tired, joyful, or grateful? These help reflect my state of mind. I hope I can correct it to make that moment the best moment ever!

Yesterday I had the best day ever. It was the weekend. Ashna and I slept in. On waking up I enjoyed a nice cup of coffee and toast with my husband, Pranav. Then we all played in the water, and I got some "me time" to be centered. I made one of my favorite meals, relished it, and food coma set in. After that, we went shopping; enjoyed the summer sun; spent some time with friends; and, at night, watched *Brooklyn*, a beautiful, thought-inspiring movie. It was a wonderful day!

Is today going to be the best day ever? Rather, am I going to make today the best day ever?

A heartfelt laugh

A tight hug

It's the best day ever

A quiet walk

A melodious tune

It's the best day ever

A long talk

A lightened heart

It's the best day ever

A naughty smile

Playful mischief

It's the best day ever

Centeredness

And a connection

It's the best day ever

A few tender moments

Summing up

To the best day ever

3. Modes of Silence

I enjoy the quiet. I enjoy stillness. I enjoy hearing the rumblings in the background and being mindful of my words and voice. As I think of quiet, I have experienced different modes of silence and thought they would be fun to share.

The first mode of silence is contemplative silence. This is when I am totally engrossed in something, when creativity flows and thoughts shape up as concrete ideas. I am focused, contemplating while being silent.

The second mode of silence is grumpy silence. For me, it comes from some trigger or expectation not met. When that happens, I feel like going into my cocoon and let the grumpy feeling pass. As my closest ones know, it can take time. Another variant of this is defensive silence. This is when, instead of responding, we go into silent mode or totally ignore the question. I have experienced this especially in e-mail communication.

The third mode of silence is quiet, meditative silence. This is when the mind or inner voice is totally quiet, and we are taking in sounds of nature or of our breath. The soul is mindful, losing all sense of time. I have experienced that during meditation. This is an enhanced state of contemplative silence. I believe that in this state, we hear messages from the universe or our higher self.

The fourth mode of silence is listening silence. This is when I am attentive and listening, trying to grasp a new concept, a different idea, and learning.

The fifth mode of silence is enforced silence. A good example of this is when we are in the library. We are expected to be silent.

The sixth mode of silence is sad silence. This is experienced when we attend funerals and when words don't seem enough to express our thoughts. Another variation of this is lonely silence. And sometimes there is painful silence.

The seventh mode of silence is awkward silence. I experience this when I am in networking events with strangers. It happens when I need to make small talk, and I run out of topics. It also happens to me when I don't remember somebody whom I am supposed to remember! We end up in awkward silence!

The eighth mode of silence is understanding silence. I see that in soul mates or friends. It is as if words are not needed to communicate. The presence is simply enjoyed. In silence, both activities and love flow.

The ninth mode of silence is when we can be silent in spite of talking or being busy in activities. This is something I have heard of. I believe that is how divine souls can continuously repeat God's name. I have not been very successful in this. The environment still impacts my being. I hope someday I can experience this mode of silence, too.

What modes of silence have you experienced?

Enjoying

The silence

And its modes

Moving from one-

To another

Connecting, Aligning, To thyself and God

I relish this quiet.

4. Fill Your Life

The thought of this came from an article in the newspaper: "Fill Your Life, Heal Your Life, Clean Your Life." I focused on the first part, "Fill Your Life." The question is, fill your life with what?

Fill your life with fun, with scriptures, with friends, with love, with happiness, with contentment, with courage, with purpose, and with faith. I think the list could go on and on. It's a fun exercise to think about what is filling up my life or what I want to fill my life with.

The next question, then, is what do you fill your time with? Are filling up your life and filling up your time separate things? Are they related?

I fill my time with work, and contentment comes along

I fill my time with family and love comes along

I fill my time with scriptures, and purpose comes along

Hence, I am very stingy when it comes to time. I protect it very strongly. I usually don't prefer going along with someone's programs just to fill time. I may go for the company or to fill my time with friends, but not just to kill time. The question is, if I am not filling my life, then what is my life being filled with?

I have observed that as life situations change, life tends to be filled with different things. Right now, as my job hunt continues, time is filled with job applications, researching companies, interview preparation, and playing the waiting game. I guess you could say: I fill my time with job applications, and I fill my life with hope.

Overall, the questions still remain: Are we true to filling our time and filling our life with things we really want? Are we centered and aligned to our life purpose? Are we living the day as the model day of our lives? Do we have enough fun things to fill our time, which will enhance life? Do we have the strong intent to "fill our lives"?

I fill my life with activity, and productivity comes along

I fill my life serving, and generosity comes along

I fill my life with writing, and wisdom comes along

I fill my life with singing, and music comes along

I fill my life with kindness, and love comes along

I fill my life with courage, and strength comes along

I fill my life with smiles, and happiness comes along

I fill my life with faith, and God comes along

5. Heal Your Life

This is part 2 of the series "Fill Your Life, Heal Your Life, and Clean Your Life." I have always believed that each one of us has our own set of challenges in life. It's like an obstacle course with lessons hidden inside. If we just look around, we can see the obstacle course, whether it's health troubles, financial issues, dissatisfaction with career or spouse, struggles to find a soul mate, family drama, or just a feeling of melancholy. The fact is, all of us have to face these, rise above them, and heal our lives.

Healing takes effort. It takes changing habits and breaking our own limiting beliefs. The saints have reminded us that we are all a part of God, and if we are centered, the obstacles won't bother us. Note, just because obstacles won't bother us doesn't mean that obstacles won't come our way. A fine example is Surdasji. He was born blind and shunned by his family. He was centered, so this didn't bother him. Rather, he had divine vision and could see more than what you and I can.

Healing needs love and compassion. As we think of the word "nurse," I am reminded of a loving mother who takes care of her children or people like Florence Nightingale. Healing our lives implies we are kind to ourselves. We stop judging; we accept what is with love and start the healing process.

Healing requires patience. Not all wounds heal quickly. The lesson is also repeated until we don't need to learn it. If a disease is recurring, maybe it's time we examine ourselves and ask: What is it that I need to learn that the universe is sending me reminders? I feel that at such times, our faith is tested; and hence, at such times, we should become even more committed to our faith.

I am a believer in using willpower and visualization to heal. We can feel sorry for ourselves for a bit, stay in that space for a little while, but then come out of it. The will to live is a powerful force. We have all been granted free will by the grace of God, and hence it's His power that we can put to use to heal ourselves. The trick is to visualize what a perfectly healthy me looks like, talks like, behaves like. Once we have that clarity, healing will follow. It is easy to see wounds on the body but harder to identify and diagnose wounds of the mind and soul. The word "heal," I believe, is derived from health. Health per WHO (the World Health Organization) is defined as physical, mental, social, and spiritual well-being. Let's heal not just physical wounds but all of these.

Healing is a noble act—whether it's for us or others. Let's heal our lives.

Wounds

Some deep

Some shallow

Some evident,

Some unknown

All of them healing

With love,

With time,

With grace

I

Observing this

Who says

Miracles don't exist?

6. Clean Your Life

This topic is part three of the series "Fill Your Life, Heal Your Life, Clean Your Life." The first thought is to physically declutter. As Lao Tzu says, *"The more frugal you are, the more generous you become."* I have an amazing feeling when I give things away. I feel release, and I feel I don't have to depend on things to make me happy. I clean my clutter, I clean my possessions, and I clean my life!

Clean your life—it means I need to be healthy and pure. I need to keep my body, my mind, and my soul clean. For the body, I kick out bad habits and focus on being healthy. This is because it's easier to be centered when we are healthy; otherwise, the mind constantly focuses on the pain or hurt. I clean my body, and I clean my life!

For the mind, I will surround myself with thoughts and people who inspire and uplift me. Energy is contagious. Just like a soiled mango can affect the surrounding good mangoes, so can bad company cover the mind with negative thoughts. I set an intention to clean my mind, and I clean my life!

For the soul, I will push to understand the mystery of the eternal truth. I will clean my soul of attachments and impressions, and I will make it pure to host the creator. Tagore captures this beautifully in Gitanjali.

Life of my life, I shall ever try to keep my body pure, knowing that thy living touch is upon all my limbs.

I shall ever try to keep all untruths out from my thoughts, knowing that thou art that truth that has kindled the light of reason in my mind.

I shall ever try to drive all evils away from my heart and keep my love in flower, knowing that thou hast thy seat in the inmost shrine of my heart.

And it shall be my endeavor to reveal thee in my actions, knowing it is thy power that gives me strength to act.

In my spiritual practice, I follow a principle called "Apras," which expresses a sense of being super clean. It implies we get clean and pure before we go in front of God. Interestingly, it talks about not just physical purity but of the mind and soul, too. So if I get angry or frustrated, I am required to go clean up again.

I am sure my husband, Pranav, will love this topic and specially that I am penning it. I tease him and call him a cleanliness freak around the home. He will say, I can finally see the light. Honestly, he is a blessing, as he reminds me of this principle while helping us have a clean home.

The purest of the pure

How can I carry you

In my tainted heart?

And yet it's your flame

That will burn these evils

And release my soul...

17

7. Empty the Boat

This thought came from the book *Dhammapada*—teachings of Buddha. As a part of my new year's resolution, I have promised to work on my patience by building more compassion. My brother recommended I review *Dhammapada*, as who else can teach us compassion and patience like Buddha? The book has various chapters of verses, and each chapter has an introduction by Eknath Easwaran.

"Empty the boat" implies getting rid of possessions. Possessions can be both material and mental. It's easier to get rid of material possessions—buying less and giving away more—though that, too, may be hard for some people. I like to keep the Japanese philosophy in mind: just in time (JIT), meaning to get things when you actually need them. Its counter philosophy is "just in case." This means I hold on to something just in case I may need it. Ironically, most times this does not work, as we forget where we have kept all these things! Let's empty our boat of material possessions.

It's harder to get rid of mental possessions—anger, irritation, greed, lust, fear, impatience, and even restlessness. Interestingly, once we give up either of these types of possessions, there is a sense of calm. I have to be careful, though, when I give up material possessions, that this does not end up as "mental" possessions—for example, I am so nice that I donated $X to this cause, and it ends up being an ego possession. Suddenly my boat is fuller than before!

"Empty the boat" is more of an inner state, an inner craving to live with just what we really need materially and spiritually. Letting go and getting rid of possessions is relieving.

What's on your boat that you would like to empty out?

Empty the boat

And let it float

Lightly

Enjoying the waves

And the rhythms

Empty the boat

Of material things

Enjoy the calmness of "Less"

Empty the boat

And let go

Of fear,

Of anger

Of greed

Empty the boat

And make space

for Him

8. Unhurried Ways

The thought of this topic was inspired by *Wayne Dyer's book, Change Your Thoughts—Change Your Life: Living the #Wisdom by Tao*. He expounds on the eighty-one verses by Lao Tzu, the ancient Chinese saint. In one of the verses, he talks about "unhurried ways." I am experiencing this phenomenon of no urgency or unhurried ways myself, as I am in job hunt mode, and I have the gift of time. As William Henry Davies magnificently puts it in his poem "Leisure":

What is this life full of care

We have no time to stand and stare

No time to stand beneath the boughs

And stare as long as sheep or cows

No time to see, when woods we pass

Where squirrels hide their nuts in grass

No time to see, in broad daylight

Streams full of stars, like skies at night

No time to turn at Beauty's glance

And watch her feet, how they can dance

No time to wait till her mouth can

Enrich the smile her eyes began

A poor life this if, full of care ....We have no time to stand and stare

I especially like my mornings with this feeling of "no urgency." Usually I am nagging Ashna to get ready quickly so we can rush out, drop her to school, and head to work. Now, it's a relaxed morning. We enjoy a few more hugs before time strikes its call! Pranav calls it a mind-set, and yes, it is one—a mind-set of enjoying time flow, enjoying being mindful, and not being captured by the clock. Lao Tzu reminds us to trust the Tao and enjoy what the universe sends our way.

The caution, however, is not to let unhurried ways lead to inertia and being lazy. Activities do expand to fit in the time. To counter this, I have made a resolution to be productive. I am confident in my ability to find fun things to fill my life.

I now see how saints live and enjoy this mind-set of unhurried ways, how they are calm and centered and how they surpass being captured by time! I believe I have to learn to truly be fully present. I am a stickler for finishing tasks (and I am sure this brings a super big smile to my brother's face, as he teases me about it all the time!). With that, my mind hovers around mundane tasks instead of enjoying these unhurried, present moments. The goal is clear: have both a mind-set of no urgency and one of being present, thus truly enjoying this moment to stand and stare.

How have you experienced unhurried ways in daily life?

A candle

Slowly burning

And

I watch

The flame

Stable and

Flickering

Alive and

Restless

Unaware of the

Light it's spreading

9. The Mandala

The thought of this topic came from watching the show *Belief* on OWN. The show was talking about Buddhist monks who have a practice called "Mandala." Mandala is a form of art using sand and stones. There are various types of Mandalas, and each has a spiritual meaning. From what I understand, it has a core and an inner and outer circle, depicting our spirit, our mind, and our circumstances/world. The idea of the Mandala is to learn to evolve from it.

The monks spend hours and hours making this beautiful art. Then, once it's done, they take a broom and, just like that, sweep it out! The lesson is that nothing is permanent, so don't get attached to your own creation. As I was watching the show, I was moved. All the hours of work to create this beautiful piece of art, and then having the courage to let it all go.

On the thought of nothing being permanent, I see it every day as I see Ashna grow. She is discovering something new every day—a new word, reading billboards, talking intelligently with our friends.

The thought of being attached to one's creation reminded me of the story of Lord Brahma (the God of creation per Hindu mythology). When the Supreme Lord asked him to create, he humbly asked for one boon—not to get attached to his own creation. He sure was wise!

I see that all the time, especially my getting attached to my creations. However, calling things "my" creations is also egoistical. I get attached to this writing, to my work, and most of all to my daughter, Ashna. Ideally, one has to be passionate about the activity, be it work or art; however, be cautious on not becoming overly attached.

Being overly attached implies that one tries to hold on things, resists change, and wants to be in control. We become fearful or insecure. Here is where "Mandala" resonates the most for me. The monks passionately work to create the best art form, concentrating, being mindful of each sand grain. Yet once it's done, they wipe it off. They have learned to control the urge of attachment and learned to change, which may mean the destruction of one's creation.

I feel once I give up being attached to things, it's relieving. It's almost as if a weight is lifted. I don't need to constantly fight to protect my creation! I learn to accept and enjoy whatever is in store for me.

What is the lesson that resonates the most for you from Mandala?

I have worked endlessly

To create

"This"

My sweat, blood and tears

Are captured in

"This"

I am in love

With

"This"

I will now

Let

"This" go

I will now

Wipe

"This" off

I will learn

To be unattached

And free

10. Do the Things That Make You Gasp

We were flying back from Bermuda. It's a beautiful, small country with a pretty pink sand beach. The water is a gorgeous blue, clear, warm, and welcoming. There I came across this thought from an article titled "Do Things That Make You Gasp."

This thought goes perfectly with my one-word resolution for the year—it's the word "courage." Doing things that make you gasp takes courage—courage to not let fear of doing it or fear of failure stop me!

The thought also hits on one of the secrets to happiness. If we do things that make us gasp, it will create more enthusiasm in our lives. A little bit of adrenaline is a good booster! But let's be cautious not to become adrenaline junkies.

The important word for me is this sentence is also the word "you." It doesn't talk about what will make the world gasp. It is saying what will make "me" gasp. The three things recently that have made me gasp are (a) quitting my job without having another one in hand, (b) traveling with my little one, Ashna, to India on standby, and (c) traveling with just hand luggage to India (to provide context, usually we would have four bags each weighing fifty pounds, and instead we came in with only carry-on bags). All of these were things I had not done ever, and all of them have made me gasp. I now have this restless but happy energy and a few butterflies, too.

Things that make you gasp can tickle, too!

A jump

A swarm of butterflies

A brake released

An unstoppable momentum

Gasps!

The energy free

Showing off

Restless and happy

I observe

I experience

I enjoy

Freedom!

11. The $10M Check

The inspiration for this story comes from one of my favorite actors, Jim Carrey. I love the scene from the movie *Bruce Almighty* where Jim Carrey becomes God for a period of time and realizes the responsibility that comes with God's power. He soon realizes that only God can handle it all, and in the scene he says, "I surrender" and is run over by a truck. The humor and trust get me every time! It eventually leads to getting his girlfriend and his job back.

The $10M check is his personal true story; he wrote himself a check for "acting services" and believed it would materialize in time. And it did! He believed and visualized and put his heart and soul into it. He believed with total intensity and integrity. His beliefs made the universe believe.

I would divide this into three things: belief, action, and grace. In the world of acronyms, I would call this a BAG—Belief, Action, and Grace—signifying the journey you are about to take! It starts with a belief, a vision, a thought. Isn't that how the universe was born? Then comes action—not just passive action but deep-seated, intense, active action to make it happen; and then finally it's grace. The $10M check then materializes! It's interesting that at this stage, it requires even more belief to acknowledge that it was your belief in yourself that was the first step to getting here.

I sometimes sell myself short. Self-doubt and "not being good enough" may haunt me, too. The first step of believing is the key. The $10M check works out for the ones who "don't stop believing." Believing not only happens for the $10M check but for also for health, for love, and for God.

What is in your BAG?

I believe

In this vision

A dream

And a reality of the future

I believe

And I act

For this dream

To make it happen

I believe

And Grace showers

My dream....Realized

In a new form...

I believe

And I surrender

To Thy will

12. Worry-Free Diet

This thought was inspired by Swami Yogananda. The message was very timely. My work has been stressful. Thankfully, we had a nice vacation planned to Puerto Rico. As I grabbed something to read, I took this pamphlet with the message "Worry-Free Diet."

The message is quite simple. As we focus on different diets to reduce weight or gain energy—protein diet, no-carb diet, liquid diet, and so on— this message is to have a "worry-free" diet. Swamiji asks us to be on a Worry-Free diet at least once a day, starting with thirty minutes, and during that time, let no worries bother us. No health worries, no work worries, no children's concerns—simply a worry-free diet.

I tried it, and it's absolutely wonderful. I didn't realize how much time I knowingly or unknowingly spent worrying, especially about minor things—how will this presentation be received? Will I be able to pick the little one up on time from day care? What will the doctor say about this pain? But for those thirty minutes, I have to make a conscious effort and practice to not worry. It feels good. The mind suddenly learns to enjoy the worry-free time! For me, my vacation further helped with inculcating it. Now, I should work on living it daily!

Will you join me in my worry-free diet?

No stress

No concerns

No fears

I am on a "worry-free" diet

This moment

Suddenly alive

Feeling the warmth

Of motherly sea

She kissed my hands

And took my worries

She showered me

With the gift of calm

The "worry-free" diet

And the bliss of peace

Accepting and enjoying .....Life's gifts

13. Let Your Heart Be Light

It's Christmas time! Radio station 93.9 Lite FM is bubbling with Christmas songs. One of them says, *"Have yourself a merry little Christmas; let your heart be light"*—inspiring this thought.

Let your heart be light—such a simple line but such a profound statement. Let no worries, fears, stress, troubles, grudges, anger, or hatred rule your heart, and let your heart be light in its weight. I have started to think of this line as any stress starts creeping in. I keep saying to myself, "Let me not drown in this feeling—let my heart be light...let my heart be light."

Another interpretation is this: Let your heart be *light*—implying that I should brighten myself and others surrounding me. Let my heart be *the light*, and let me light others' hearts and souls. It can be through simple things—a word of encouragement, a kind word, an acknowledgment of things well done, or simply a smile.

As this Christmas Day springs upon me, I promise to let my heart be light.

Are you promising that, too?

My heart

Light

As a feather

Buoyant

Soaring

Enjoying the wind

My heart

Lighting up

My path

And yours

A tiny nudge

Let my heart be light

Today and

Every day

14. Cut It Out!

The thought of this chapter is inspired by the series *Full House*, spoken by the character Joey. The thought is further built up by many books, too, one of them being *The Man Who Sold His Ferrari* by Robin Sharma. The crux is that if I begin my thought chain of blaming somebody, complaining, or dwelling on something negative, I simply should "cut it out." Don't encourage it. Don't let it grow. Consciously and cautiously let me "cut it out."

As we may all have noticed—I certainly have—negative thoughts are a rabbit hole. Whether it's fear, whether it's finding fault, or whether it's plain gossiping, at the end, I feel it leaves me with a lower mind-set, a grumpy mind-set. The key is "cut it out." It's weird how both complaining and gratitude work and how they spread into everything. I start complaining about something little, and very soon I find faults in everything—the sun is too hot, the traffic on the roads is too loud, and so on. Very soon it starts showing itself in your demeanor. If, instead, I foster a sense of gratitude, it also spreads; and pretty soon I am thankful for everything—a new day, a nice warm day, activity depicted by traffic on the road, and liveliness within.

A different thought is that if you are feeling negative, be in the feeling and get out of it. It's the opposite idea of "cut it out." Somehow I can't relate to that fully. "Cut it out" is what I feel is my mantra. As I catch myself grumbling, I focus on the mantra and try to dwell on happy thoughts. The more I "cut it out," the more I feel closer to my true self. Thanks, Joey!

What's on your "cut it out" list?

Finger pointing

Complaints

Pettiness

Cut it out!

Holding it on and on

Greed and anger

Cut it out!

Temptations and lethargy

A dullness

Cut it out!

"I" am right there

Cut this veil out

And let me in

Let me in

15. Love Your Neighbor, but First Love Yourself

This thought was inspired from a rerun of Oprah Winfrey's show. She was interviewing three young adults, each addicted to plastic surgeries. The young woman, twenty-eight years old, has had twenty-three plastic surgeries! A few nose jobs; lifting cheeks; liposuction of tummy, thighs; brow lift; and so on. Funnily she was pretty even before she got all the surgeries. Honestly, she looked artificial—like a Barbie doll. She still didn't like her reflection in the mirror. Hence the thought, "Love thy neighbor, but first love yourself."

The common theme among all those women addicted to plastic surgeries was exactly this: they kept seeing imperfections in their reflections. They were not able to accept their own selves. They were willing to go through the pain of surgery and recovery with the illusion that this one would get them back to being "OK" with themselves.

It was quite surprising—and sad. I had always taken for granted that everyone loves at least his or her own self. It's easier, in my opinion, to love others and love our neighbors if we start with ourselves. As Zoe Kravitz says, *"Beauty is when you can appreciate yourself. When you love yourself, that's when you're most beautiful."*

Most scriptures and saints talk about feeling the love for everybody as a stage of enlightenment. First you love yourself, then your neighbors, then the community, then the city, then the nation, and then the world...slowly your love expands to everybody!

I do believe loving yourself is important. Imagine—otherwise, we would be spending all our time doubting and criticizing ourselves. The caution is not to become a narcissist. The caution is also to have deep humility. Everything needs to be balanced!

In conclusion, I feel the first step is to love oneself. Let me not be fooled by my image or reflection and get into the tireless endeavor to perfect it. I will start with acceptance. One of these days, with deep humility, I hope to evolve to loving my neighbor!

My reflection laughs at me

What have I done!

In the desire to look good

I lost myself

I start again with acceptance

I love me…I really love me

For what I am

With deep humility

I start this journey

To expand my love

…to you …to everybody

Searching and bowing to the God

Within us

"Namaste"

16. Ten Thousand Ears

The inspiration for this topic is the story of King Prithu from Shrimad Bhagwat, a Hindu religious scripture. King Prithu did a lot of penance, and as a result, God appeared before him. God asked him to ask a boon. The king requested ten thousand ears to hear God's praises and Satsang. Satsang is defined as company with an assembly of persons who listen to, talk about, and assimilate the truth.

The orator, Satish Sharma, who was explaining this story, mentioned that we all hear things that we either remember or forget. If we hear with our two ears, we may forget, but if we hear with all our ten thousand ears, we will remember.

As I reflected on it, I wondered, what have I heard with ten thousand ears? I know harsh words are up there! Those, I wish I would have heard with just two ears to forgive and forget. On the other hand, I wish I would have paid even more attention and heard the scriptures with ten thousand ears. I am sure that would help me experience God.

What have you heard with your ten thousand ears?

Ten thousand ears

And my mind

Hearing

Ignoring

Listening

Focusing

Living

Ten Thousand ears

And distractions

Listening and repeating

Over and over

Yet, it's our ears

And our choice

To keep it in

Or throw it out

17. The Practice of Forgiveness

Once upon a time there was a teacher—a Tao guru—and his student. The student had a bad habit of holding grudges against people. The guru told him to carry a big bag of potatoes for a week. At the end of the week, the student showed up with an aching back and some smelly potatoes. The teacher mentioned that when we carry ill will in our heart, this is what happens. The heart becomes heavy, and the conscious self-shows signs of staling. The guru then asked the student if in the past week he had developed any other ill feelings, and the student realized the trap he had built for himself. The art of forgiveness is the trick to breaking the shackles of ill feelings.

Luckily, so far, I am blessed to have no major grudges against people. The art of forgiveness is sure easy with minor grudges! However, I have seen people up close who hold on to things for such a long time. A wife, separated for the last twenty years, still complaining about her husband. A daughter-in-law, now seventy years old, bringing up grudges against her mother-in-law that are decades old. However, I have also met a person who daily, in his prayers, thinks about people he may likely hold grudges against and prays for their well-being. He, for sure, is teaching the art of forgiveness.

As someone has said, forgiving somebody is a gift you give yourself. Imagine the purity and peace we would have if we had no bitterness. For that moment that we reminisce about the painful past, we lose this moment, too, and we lose the chance to be centered.

As I watch myself, I try to reinforce the art of forgiveness. Join me in the effort to master this art!

No complaints

No grudges

No bitterness

It's all in the past

I have moved on

And so has he

His thoughts…those events

Are just ghosts of the past

Claiming my present

I own my present

I choose to forgive

For my sake!

18. Let the Loop Run Itself Out

This topic is based on an interview on *Super Soul Sunday*, one of my favorite TV shows. The interview was with Dr. Jill Bolte Taylor, author of the book *The Stroke of Insight*, on her experience after suffering a massive stroke and loss of function in the left hemisphere of her brain. So, she started using her right hemisphere. This hemisphere helps us see the bigger picture, and as Pranav observed, in meditation we want the right hemisphere to lead us instead of the ego-self of the left hemisphere.

With the stroke of insight as she calls it, she was talking about anger and asked us all to "let the loop run itself out." For most negative emotions, it takes ninety seconds for chemicals to be generated and released. If we could just let ninety seconds pass and let the loop run out, we would technically control our reactions. Dr. Jill further elaborated that people can be angry for years, as they may recall a bad memory, thus triggering the loop to begin again.

I have a lot to learn from this. I do get triggered and I do get angry. Hence, my lessons are (a) let the loop run out and (b) train your thoughts not to trigger the loop. I do have a clear sense of self-awareness and repentance as I get caught in the loop.

I really like Wayne Dyer's quote *"I have infinite patience"*. For me that is my guru mantra.

Let the loop run itself out!

Ninety seconds

Is all I ask

To let the loop run out

Ninety seconds

Of forbearance

Of control

Of patience

Of forgiveness

Of love

Ninety seconds

...A lifetime

To let the loop run out

19. The Feeling of Self-Reliance

The thought of this topic was inspired from the movie *Still Alice*. It is about a woman struggling with the early onset of Alzheimer's disease. In a scene, she was trying to set a reminder on her phone for her daughter's recital. Most of her family asked her not to bother—they would ensure she attended the recital. However, the daughter encouraged it—encouraged the feeling of self-reliance.

I feel that in disease, other than physical discomfort, it is the feeling of dependence that bothers us. My husband's grandma, Ba, as we call her, is nearing ninety. As I hear her speak and reminisce about her life, it is evident that she misses being self-reliant. Funnily, I see the same with my daughter, Ashna. When she was three she learned to put on her PJs, and she wanted to do it herself. It bothered her if we try to help! The feeling of self-reliance knows no age boundaries!

I am a believer in self-reliance—physically, mentally, financially, and spiritually. I feel I have made very conscious choices to stay self-reliant. For example, financially, I have consciously chosen to be a working mom so that I can be self-reliant. For mental and spiritual self-reliance, I read the works of Swami Vivekananda and Swami Yogananda, who help reinforce courage of the mind and power of the will to encourage self-reliance, amongst other things.

Finally we come to "s" and "S" of self-reliance. I am reliant on Self. I trust He has my best interest, and I trust Him to direct this life at His will. One of these days, or one of these lifetimes, the small self will merge into Self—I will be truly Self-reliant!

"I do myself" says my little one

Learning self-reliance

"I can't do myself" says my grandma

Grieving self-reliance

"I can do myself" says my ego

Boasting self-reliance

"I should do myself" says my husband

Pushing self-reliance

Let the Self rule

Says my self

Trusting "Self" Reliance

20. The Tyranny of "Should"

The thought of this topic came from an article in the *Business Insider* on a psychologist's discovery of how not to get frustrated. One of the key reasons he cited was the "tyranny of should." "I should have had that promotion"; "She should clean up her mess"; "This work should have been done"; or "I should have behaved a certain way." The tyranny of should, in short, is the difference between expectations and reality.

I have been a victim of this tyranny! Just last week, I had a long discussion—or rather, a venting session—and it came down to the gap between my expectations and reality. Oh, the tyranny of should!

How do we then stop this tyranny? A few thoughts—change the "should" to "could." What could I do? How can I help resolve? Let "could" fight "should."

The tyranny of should also occurs, in my case, when I don't clarify my expectations and have unrealistic deadlines. Let open communication fight the tyranny of should.

Lastly, it is what it is. Acceptance is the key here. If I can change something, let me do it. If it's not possible, let it be. I will accept it. Let acceptance fight the tyranny of should.

One of these days, I will conquer the tyranny of should. How have you fought this?

Mighty expectations

Unsaid words

The tyranny of "Should" rises

All the imaginations

And bitter reality

The "Should" tyrant dances

What should be done?

What could I do?

What could I say?

What could I accept?

With the sword of could

I fight the tyranny of should

21. Ignorance and Innocence

This topic was inspired by Ashna. It has been a fun experience to see her grow, discover things, and develop her personality. Ashna, like other children, showcases innocence. Thinking about ignorance, I am not much into current affairs; and recently, in a conversation, I acknowledged my ignorance.

Innocence comes from a clean heart and a trusting nature. In innocence, we accept things as they seem. Ironically, in innocence, we are closer to God. As we get "smarter," we start building barriers, bringing more of our rational selves into the picture—maybe becoming more ignorant. Does innocence at one point lead to ignorance?

Ignorance, on the other hand, is where we don't know or where the intellect is not fast or smart enough to grasp the meaning. It's easier to fix the "we don't know" part. It's harder and takes more effort to push the intellect. The story that comes to mind is that of Panini. He became an excellent scholar in Sanskrit grammar and is known for writing multiple scriptures. However, when he was young, he had a really hard time learning and memorizing verses. He was taunted and rebuked by his peers and teachers. At one point, he planned to commit suicide by jumping into a well. By God's grace he saw some ladies drawing out water from a well. He noticed how the rope had created grooves in the well's wall. He decided that if the wall could get grooves through repetition, his mind could, too. With new enthusiasm, he returned, and over time, he become a world-renowned scholar.

For innocence, I think of the verse, *"Give me the pureness, clarity, and transparency of glass; then I will imbibe Your name in my heart."*

For ignorance, I remember Panini and also caution myself to be aware of my ignorance getting in the way of spiritual progress.

Innocence

Ultimate trust

Unassuming?

Accepting the Is

Ignorance

Not knowing,

Not questioning

What is possible

I pray for

Childlike innocence

To love Thee

And Challenge the ignorance

To know Thee

22. Tough Lives of God

This topic was inspired as I was reading Shrimad Bhagwat, a Hindu scripture. The scripture talks about all twenty-four incarnations of God and stories of his devotees. As I was looking and contemplating God's life in the incarnations, it is obvious that these are very tough lives! It's the same theme if you see Jesus Christ's life.

Think about Shri Ram spending fourteen years in the jungle, fighting demons; or Shri Krushna, who was attacked by demons when he was a baby; or Christ and the crucifixion. Even gods aren't spared! Would you like to trade in the life you have for the lives of these gods? In the true sense of love, you would trade in all pains if it relieves your beloved.

Everyone faces tough times in life. Sometimes these are external. We continue to hear news about people fleeing from a country to avoid violence or poverty. Thankfully, all of us in the United States or in peaceful countries are blessed, and we don't have to worry about that, at least from external circumstances; we are not in the midst of war or poverty.

Recently, many of my close friends have been going through their own tough times, either with disease or with death. At such times, I am reminded of devout followers of God—specifically Prahlad. He was five years old and already very devoted to God. His father opposed his devotion tremendously and tried various methods to get rid of that devotion. When that didn't work, the father tried to kill Prahlad. God protected his devotee in each of the calamities. Interestingly, Prahlad never asked God for mercy. He never asked God to save him from misery or harm his father. Prahlad just continued to chant God's name. With each calamity, his intensity of devotion increased.

I wonder if I could have kept my devotion intact, or if I would have blamed God or begged God for mercy. Tough times didn't sway Prahlad; rather, they helped him to be even more focused on God.

For me, it's a great reminder that everyone faces tough periods in life—whether it's God or his devotees. With toughness of will, the Grace of God, and steadfast devotion, this too shall pass.

A rough day

Tough years

And these too shall pass

Steadfast devotion, Strong will and Laser sharp focus

These…I will bring

Grace and More Grace

Is all I will need

Let me be centered

Help me increase my intensity

Of devotion

Let tough times

Remind me and lead me

To Thee

23. Not Who—But Why?

The thought for this chapter came from a training on EQ (emotional quotient). It talked about how we need to be aware of our perceptions. It further talked about how to "seek to understand," thus reinforcing not who but why.

Let me cite an example. I work with someone who seemed like a naysayer. She would find all the reasons something wouldn't work or complicate a simple process with a bombardment of questions. This was my initial perception. As I got to know her better, I realized that she is very detailed and likes thinking through all the scenarios. As she is detailed, she expects the team to think through all potential roadblocks. The "why" is her need for clarity on details, and the "who" is being who she is!

Sometimes my "judgmental" personality comes into play, and I have to try harder to ask the questions and understand the context. I also enjoy the "speed" of doing things, and roadblocks like this ensure I learn the art of patience.

The reminder is "not who but why." What is the context? Why is the person asking the question? What is bothering him or her? What is he or she scared of? What is his or her intent? Let's seek to understand a different point of view.

Not who but why

Ask the question

Let go of the perception

And seek to understand

Not who but why

Explain the context

Open up and

Give the why

Not who but why

Align on the purpose

And start there

It's the why

That holds the keys

To open the door

24. Identity Crisis

It all started when we had a massive layoff in our department. It came as a surprise. The gentleman who was impacted had eighteen years of tenure with the company. His identity was defined by his work at this company. His reaction, naturally, was one of disbelief. He was facing an identity crisis!

I have always believed that our identity should not be solely dependent on our work. We should have different facets to our identity. I am blessed to have different hobbies that help me expand my perspective and the people I interact with. Hence, they help expand my identity as an earthly being. However, it's still limiting as now I am limited to my identity with my hobbies.

It's also interesting to view identity from external and internal perspectives. Most people, including me at times, start believing that the perception people have about us is true. However, true identity is how we think of ourselves. What is the mirror telling me?

As we think further on identity, I am reminded of Sri Sri Ravishankar. He asks, "Who am I?" Are you Ms. ABC? Are you the body, or are you the soul? "Who am I?" is a perennial question, and it's amazing to introspect on the different answers that come to mind. He further asks us to contemplate on the question, "Where am I?"—going from the microlevel of each DNA strand in the cell to the macrolevel of a miniscule part of the entire universe. I am reminded of the Sanskrit Verse *"Nirvana Shatkam."*

I am not mind, intellect, ego and the memory. I am not the sense organs (ears, tongue, nose, eyes and skin). I am not the five elements (sky, earth, fire, wind and water). I am supreme bliss and pure consciousness, I am Shiva, I am all auspiciousness, I am Shiva.

I had read a story of a saint whom someone asked, "Who are you?" His response was, "A servant of the Almighty." I guess if your identity is linked back to the infinite and the limitless, there is no scope of identity crisis.

Who are you, again?

The boss called me

And thanked me for my services

I am fired

I am free

And "I" am lost

The pursuit begins

To find the path

To recreate "me"

The same fallacy

The same mistake

I need to break

The barriers

That limit me!

25. What Are You Going to Do Less Of and More Of?

As the New Year begins, I enjoy reflecting on the past year—rating and noting key events of the year in material and spiritual terms. At that time, I revisit my resolutions and evaluate those, too. As I started thinking about them for the New Year, it inspired this topic: What am I going to do more of and less of?

In the past years, I had "activity"-based resolutions. I will exercise three times a week, I will spend more time practicing music, and so on. Then last year my coach, Marian Baker, gave great advice. She said to think about how you want to "feel," and that will drive the right behavior or activities. She did warn, though, that we need to continue to remind ourselves and focus of how we want to feel and whether this activity will help us move toward it or away from it. So last year, my resolutions were that I want to feel healthier and have more stamina, and I want to feel recharged through music.

This year I decided to take a twist on this and ask the question: "What I will do less of, and what I will do more of? I also decided to just come up with three core things to work on: less overreaction, more meaningful activity (fewer wasteful activities), and more time in spiritual pursuits. I have decided to focus on each quarter and take up the twenty-one-day challenges. The first three months involve mastering less overreaction, and the twenty-one-day challenge is...no complaining (http://www.acomplaintfreeworld.org/). Physically, I have a ninety-day challenge to lose five to seven pounds.

What are you going to do less of and more of?

A year gone

A time to reflect

A time to resolve

A time to see time move

A subtle realization

Archiving the year … In totality?

A struggle

To undo the past from the present

A new year

Can be a new life

Changes and challenges

Enthusiasm and apprehension

In the end it's up to us

With the gift of free will

To do or undo another year

57

26. Leave the Driving to Greyhound

This line was phrased by my brother, Dr. Anurag, in one of our conversations on surrendering to God's will. It's easier for us to accept someone else being in the driver's seat when we are in a train or a plane. In a car, though, I, for sure, am a backseat driver, or I tend to hold the windowsill—as if that is really going to protect me in case of a crash.

"Leave the driving to Greyhound" implies that we surrender, and we trust. We accept that God knows what's best for us, and we walk on the path without resisting or doubting. We let our will align to his will.

In the Hindu scriptures, we read that God has two kinds of children: those who are wise and who can take care of themselves and those who are childlike and need God to take care of them. They are compared to child-monkeys who have to take effort and responsibility to cling to their mothers whereas the latter are young kittens that are lifted by the mouth by their cat mother till they can move about on their own. God pays less attention to the wise children. For the childlike ones, he is always there, protecting and caring. From Pushti-marg Vaishnav's mind-set of the servant or lover mentality, we don't want to be a further bother to God. However, we want—seriously want—to feel His presence. Does that mean we should be like his wise children? Or can I be a childlike devotee without being annoying? Whatever type of devotee I am at a moment, I need to remember to "leave the driving to Greyhound" and accept all that God has designed for me to experience.

You drive and I'll ride

Wherever you take me

Whenever you take me

However you take me

You drive and I'll ride

I know and I trust

You know the path

And you know the destination

You drive and I'll ride

I promise

Not to be a backseat driver

Not to question your judgment

I promise to accept

You drive and I'll ride

In surrender and in love

27. Courage and Resilience

The thought for this topic arose from *Super Soul Sunday* with the story of Whole Foods CEO John Mackey. At one point in his life, somehow he became very conscious of life being short, and he decided to live and do the things he really wanted to do. He was in school at that time. He took up various electives, things he really wanted to learn, but didn't complete his education. With courage and confidence, he followed the path—the path of doing what one really wants to do.

As I think of my life, it points more to resilience. At age of sixteen, I decided to pursue courses in science, and I struggled. It wasn't the right fit, but I kept at it. During my career, too, there have been roles that weren't a fit or roles that, after some time, didn't seem to fit. I kept at it, too, with resilience. I waited for the perfect time to get out—the low-risk method.

Courage also reminds me of Maya Angelou, who considered courage to be the prime value. It is courage that gives us strength to follow our dreams and live by our ideals. And it's resilience that helps us not quit when the road gets harder. I would argue that resilience also requires strength and courage. However, I would also argue that if your heart tells you it's the wrong path, you should have the courage to take the risk and quit. Dear God, help me have the courage to identify and walk on the path and the resilience to keep at it.

What do you think? Do you lean more toward courage or resilience?

I have the courage to follow my dreams

And I have the resilience to walk the path

I have the courage to take it on

And I have the resilience to keep at it

I have the courage to trust

And I have the resilience to love

I have the courage to seek You

And the resilience to not quit

28. The Gratitude Journal

This topic was inspired by the book *Happiness Project* and further inspired by my husband, Pranav. The thought is that each day, you note three things you are grateful for—and it must be three different things every day. As you continue to do this, it becomes a habit. Eventually it leads to realization and acknowledgment of our blessings. Pranav follows this advice and has his own Gratitude Journal.

I have tried this mentally (and I need to make it a practice to have my own journal, too). Funnily, I have to really think before I note the 3 things. The expectations even from a Gratitude Journal are high!

As I snoop and read Pranav's journal, I am amazed to see how thankful he is for very simple things—a good meal, playful times with Ashna, or ever a simple hug or good beer.

The learning for me is the mindfulness of being thankful for the daily, taken-for-granted things. We don't have to win a lottery every day to be thankful! What should I *not* be grateful for?

I am grateful for this moment

A quiet morning

This journal

And the brewing coffee

I am grateful for

This longing…A deep urge

This curiosity

And chirping birds

I am grateful for

Those tiny hands holding me tight

A naughty smile and a stubborn mind

I am grateful for

Even those unpleasant moments

That remind me

To continue this journey

I am grateful for

You and Him

And Us

I am deeply grateful

29. The Conditions for Happiness

The thought for this chapter started from reading the book *The Untethered Soul*, by Michael Singer. The author explains that we keep conditions for our happiness. "I will be happy if I am promoted," or "I will be happy if I get married / pregnant." He believes that we should instead focus on unconditional happiness. It sure made me think. I myself had said, "Happiness is a state after the fulfillment of one desire and before the birth of another."

While talking with my colleague Maggie, I found that she believes competition and winning are inculcated in our minds. We tend to link achievement to happiness. The question she raised was, "How will we keep ourselves motivated if we delink happiness and success?"

Coincidentally, Pranav came across a book called *Happiness Project* in which the author says that happiness begets success instead of success leading to happiness. I believe the thought is that as we become more happy, the calmness and joy show in our work, leading to success.

A higher state of mind is when we are above all this to enjoy unconditional happiness—being happy just because it's our true nature or the nature of God. I have spent a long time building conditions on my happiness and linking achievement and happiness. I think it's time to let go and work on being unconditionally happy and blissful.

Have you put conditions on your happiness, too?

Let success be condition based

Let happiness just exist

Be happy no matter what

Be happy for you

For us

For Him

Be happy today

Right now

Let that smile shine

Your day and mine

Be happy

It's a command

And a blessing

(Last three lines quoted from Sri Sri Ravishankar)

30. No Big Deal

This topic was inspired by my husband, Pranav. Let me paint the picture. I typically get up around 5:00 to 5:30 a.m., but I take my own sweet time to get ready—usually by 7:30 a.m. So, on the days when I have an earlier business meeting, I get edgy. I start rushing things, becoming short and making it into a "big deal." Pranav, on the other hand, goes with the flow. He has to take a 6:00 a.m. flight pretty regularly. He takes it easy after getting up at 3:30 a.m.! He is calm and happy, and it's "no big deal." I need to, and am trying to, learn that it's "no big deal"!

My friend calls this a first-world problem. She is so right that we make small things that can and should be ignored into this mammoth endeavor. It's no big deal!

I often remember the story of a particular gentleman. His day didn't start right. The alarm didn't go off. He was late. Being edgy, he spilled his coffee on himself. Finally, after he got out of the house, he got stuck in traffic, further delaying him. The anxious energy was rising. Suddenly he saw the accident. That was what was delaying the traffic. And things came into perspective. He was alive. He was well. He had a nice family, a decent job, and good health. Being late one day was "no big deal"!

I remind myself to keep things in perspective, to count my blessings, to be grateful for all we have, and let things go. It's really "no big deal."

"No big deal" is Pranav's motto

"Let it go" is Ashna's

"Be happy" says my mom

"Laugh it out" is mine

"It doesn't matter" reinforces my dad

"Forgive" advises Daddu [father-in-law]

"Beat it" showcases Mumma [mother-in-law]

"It's God's desire "acknowledges my bro

"Accept the change" calls out sis-in-law

"Drive" says bro-in-law

"It's all good" reminds my friend

"Live in grace" guides the Guru

"Trust me"

Smiles my God

✶✶✶✶✶✶✶✶✶✶✶✶✶✶

Made in the USA
Monee, IL
07 May 2023